We Blazed The Trail

Motoring to Yellowstone in Mike Dowling's Oakland!

By Dorothy Dowling Prichard

as told to Barry Prichard

Best wishes Nancy

"Har det bra!"

Barry Prichard

Published by Richards Publishing Co., PO Box 159, Gonvick, MN 56644
Phone 218-487-5225 • 444-9258 • Fax 218-487-5251
E-mail: richards@gvtel.com

Cover design and maps by Jessica Wike
Photographs restored and enhanced by Picture This, Bemidji, MN

Publisher's Cataloging in Publication

We Blazed the Trail: Motoring to Yellowstone in Mike Dowling's Oakland, by
Dorothy Dowling Prichard as told to Barry Prichard

1. Yellowstone Trail Association (U.S.)
2. Automobile Travel (U.S.)
3. Automobiles - History - GM Oakland/Pontiac
4. Minnesota History - Michael J. Dowling
5. Yellowstone Trail - History

Library of Congress Control Number 2008940105

ISBN 978-0-9759180-0-5

First Edition December 2008

Printed in the United States of America

ACKNOWLEDGEMENTS

This is a book of wonderful memories which were told to me or passed along in letters, writings and conversations with my mother, Dorothy Dowling Prichard who died on December 4, 1997, having reached the golden age of 99 years.

Heartfelt appreciation to my wife, Joan, for her unending support. Warmest thanks to my brother, my aunts, my cousins and other family members for their recollections. Thanks as well to Jack Windhorst and Adrian Bottge for their contributions. And, to Jane Rice, Mary Lou Smith, Bill Dirnberger, Alice and John Ridge, Blair Younger, Stephen Hamlin, Bruce Cortis, Lance Sorenson, Darla Jares and all of the particularly helpful editors, librarians, genealogists, historians and automobile enthusiasts of every description who offered assistance. Thanks to all for your good help and encouragement!

Dorothy Dowling Prichard at age 94.

A VERY SPECIAL THANKS....

Very special thanks to Ross Walkup, who took me for a 300-mile "run" in his vintage 1913 Oakland 6-60 touring car and actually allowed me to drive it for a couple of miles over an unpaved, gravel road.

BARRY PRICHARD is a Captain, U.S. Naval Reserve (Retired) who lives by a lake in northern Minnesota.

Contents

INTRODUCTION

Almost 100-years ago, Michael J. Dowling, my grandfather, led three families on a "first time by automobile" adventure run and blazed the way for building one of the first highways across America.

Michael Dowling was an incredible human being! At age 14, he was frozen and nearly died in the great Minnesota blizzard of 1880. Doctors amputated both feet, one hand and all fingers from the other hand. "Thank God, I'm not a cripple!" he often declared. Young Michael refused to live on welfare and worked to become a successful teacher, editor, banker, politician, foreign envoy, nationally known public speaker and more! His courage and achievements were a wonder and inspiration to people everywhere. But, nothing he attempted seems more unimaginable, today, than the historic trip he led, marking the route of the Yellowstone Trail, America's first coast-to-coast automobile highway across the northern states.

Dowling was first to reach Yellowstone by automobile from Minneapolis-St. Paul

When the "horseless carriage" was invented, Dowling was the first in Renville County to buy one in April 1903. He loved driving it everywhere around his home in Olivia, Minnesota and sometimes as far as to Minneapolis and back. But in those days, horses still outnumbered automobiles. Streets were still lighted by gas lamps and many rural towns and villages were just beginning to get electricity. Then, in 1913, he acquired a big, impressive GM Oakland 6-60 touring car. And, soon afterwards announced at the dinner table that he was taking the family, children included, on a trip westward by car to Yellowstone Park.

Riding in the open car would be his lovely wife, Jennie (Bordewich) Dowling, and their three young daughters. My mother Dorothy or "Dode" was the oldest of the Dowling girls. Following in a caravan would be Mr. and Mrs. James Empey, driving a 1912 Ford and six members of the William Windhorst family in a somewhat over-loaded 1911 Buick.

The long drive to Yellowstone quickly became an exhausting endurance test of cars, drivers and passengers. Dowling's Oakland was the only car with a self starter or electric headlights. The other cars had to be hand-cranked and had gas headlamps. Water was dripped onto calcium carbide pellets in a device on the running board, to generate acetylene gas. Car engines often over-heated and radiators needed water. There were no paved highways and only about 120 miles of improved gravel roads along the way. Most of the driving was on grassy horse and wagon trails, through fences and along soft and muddy farm roads. In some places there was not even a trace of ruts in the dirt, but only a sea of prairie grass! There were rivers and streams to cross and no bridges or signs to follow. My grandfather planned to blaze some stretches by marking trees, poles or rocks with yellow paint.

The great purpose of the trip was to show that the dream of family travel by automobile had become reality and to make headlines for the proposed new Yellowstone Trail and the growing movement for America to build "A Good Road from Plymouth Rock to Puget Sound."

The accompanying photographs are enlarged reproductions selected from my mother's 1913 snapshot album of this historic first trip by auto over the Yellowstone Trail. All of her photos were taken with her Kodak "Brownie" camera. This is her story as passed along and told to me.

BARRY PRICHARD

1913

WEST TO YELLOWSTONE

OFF WE GO....INTO THE WILD, WILD WEST!

It all began one evening in June of 1913 while we were seated around the family dinner table at our house on DePue Avenue in Olivia, Minnesota. In those days, most families sat together for meals. So, we were all in the formal dining room with its built-in china cupboards, crystal chandelier and swinging door to the pantry. Dad was at one end of the large table between Aunt Hattie and my sister Marjorie. Mother sat at the opposite end, nearest the kitchen, between Gram Bordewich and my little sister Kathleen. We called her Kay and she was only 5-years old at the time. I was sitting on one side, in the middle, where I could look out the big windows and see the lawn and driveway and the buckthorn trees and elms and some of Mother's peonies. Mother came to the table, sat for a minute and urged everyone, "Let's all take our time and not hurry!"

The next thing we knew, Dad was telling one of his wondrous tales in which he pictured our family traveling like pioneers through the wild west, in the spirit of Lewis and Clark, on our way to Yellowstone National Park. "Imagine riding through the park in a carriage and four," he enthused," with a guide to show us the geysers and hot springs, lakes and waterfalls, bears and wildlife! And, at the end of the day enjoying a relaxed stay at one of the park's grand hotels."

"We can drive there in the Oakland," he said. "It should only take 7-days and that is a good, comfortable car."

Our family was Irish-Norwegian by heritage, so I probably wondered if he was talking Irish blarney, or what? But, Dad made it sound so wonderful that I began to imagine that it really could be an exciting family vacation and summertime trip.

"And, my darlings," Father continued, "we'll be the first to blaze a route across 5-states for what will someday become a great automobile highway extending from coast to coast."

"Is this about politics, then?" Hattie asked. She was Mother's sister and lived with us for ages.

Papa shook his head. "We're simply going to show that ordinary families with children can now travel anyplace, anytime, in any kind of automobile for less than the fare by rail." You have to remember that in those days, railroads were all powerful and held a virtual monopoly on the movement of freight and mail and travel in general. And, he was against that.

I could tell by her manner that Mother still had some doubts. "What if the car breaks down and nobody knows where to find us?" she asked.

"Don't worry, my dearest Jennie," Father soothed, "we won't be driving alone. The Windhorsts want to come with us in their 1911 Buick and Jim Empey and his bride want to come, too, in their 1912 Ford. Empey can replace a fan belt or help with any repairs. He's really pretty handy." Our family knew the Empeys well. Mr. Empey was manager of the elevator and Mrs. Empey was a good friend of Mother's from church and the "Just Six" club.

"How is Bill Windhorst able to drive all that way?" Mother wondered. Her brother Harald was married to Flora, one of the Windhorst daughters. Mr. Windhorst owned a prosperous lumberyard, but Mother had been told he was a drinker. She never doubted whether Dad could drive that far and none of us thought Dad was a cripple!

"Not to worry," Dad said. "Their son, Oscar, the one everybody calls "Boss" will be driving for the Windhorsts. And, I really like that young blade!"

"Papa, will you let me drive some of the way?" I pleaded. "I'm almost 15. You said that's old enough to drive."

Dad thought for a minute, and told me, "Not until you can jack up that big car and change and patch a tire by yourself. But, on this trip, you can be my mechanic in charge of watching the thermometer on the radiator and making sure we don't lose our tools again. If we lose our big hex wrench, we won't be able to open the gasoline tank."

"What will I be?" my sister Marjorie wanted to know. "You can be our jester, keep the maps and be my secretary," Dad teased.

"Will it be like a covered wagon trail?" Kay wondered. "Will we have to camp out in tents?"

"No, my dear, we won't be camping rough. Most of the trail is mapped or marked. We'll usually be near a railroad and there are towns along the line with hotels or rooming houses or places to stay for a night."

"It's going to be boring," Kay objected as she fidgeted at the table and looked away. But, going anywhere with Papa was never boring.

"You can snooze if there's nothing to see," Dad told Kay, "but, we may go through some Indian villages and cowboy ranches like your Papa worked at when he was a boy. And, you'll want to be wide awake to see the bears at Yellowstone."

"Are you sure we can drive over the mountains in a car?" Mother persisted.

"That's my plan," Dad nodded. "The Yellowstone Trail Association has already created a lot of good road through the Dakotas and they are using convict labor to blast through the rocks and make roads over the mountains in Montana. I'm optimistic that we'll make it there safely."

Gram Bordewich had been living with us since Grandpa died in Norway the year before. She was born in Lofoten, still grieving and dressed severely, but wore a beautiful, large silver pin to liven up her dress. When she was upset with the rest of us, she sometimes went for days speaking only to Dad. She thought he was "king," That evening, as I recall, she said something in Norwegian (Du vil mistet veien! Hvem vill finne du?), asked to be excused and climbed upstairs to her own room and treasures on the 3rd floor.

"She won't be left at home alone." Dad observed in a kindly voice. "Hattie will be here, too, as well as the housekeeper. (For the life of me, I can't remember if that was Lizzie from England or Betsy from Norway or someone else?) Dad looked at Hattie. "You and Harald can take care of business and run the bank while I am away. And, Gram and the neighbors will watch the house. I wouldn't want anybody taking books out of our library before I have read them. Mr. Jackson and Tom Noske will take care of the cow and horse and keep the barn and mow the lawn."

Ours was a household dominated by women and girls, but ruled by my father. He was quite strict with me about whom I could be with and when to be home. Marjorie got by more easily. I'm sure that all of us adored Dad. But with Hattie it sometimes went too far. She was Mother's unmarried younger sister, Dad's good right hand in business and politics and an officer of the bank. Sometimes she tried to take charge of the house and the discipline of us girls, too, much to the annoyance of Mother and of us. The Oakland was a full sized touring car, but I was probably just as glad she wouldn't be riding with us.

"When are you planning to leave?" Mother finally asked.

"Not until after the Independence Day parade," Father decided. "Dorothy and the girls can see that the car is washed and shined right down to the tires and decorated with flags and banners for that grand celebration. Then, we'll allow a day to get packed and loaded. I'll tell the Windhorsts and Empeys to be ready to leave early July 6th. That's a Sunday morning."

"Be sure to pack a picnic basket and a box of apples and fruit on the running board." Kay exclaimed.

And so it was decided that we would really go on that historic trek. Mother invited all of the "Yellowstone Bunch" (There were 13 of us) to an early breakfast at the Dowling house. After which, skipping church and ignoring superstition, we rolled out of town in single file, on our way to Yellowstone, with Father driving and leading the way.

Looking back, I saw Hattie and Gram, Uncle Harald and Flora and several of our close neighbors out on their front lawns, waving goodbye. Everybody was in a happy, festive mood. I think somebody's dog chased us out of town. If we only knew what lay ahead!

OUR 1913 OAKLAND TOURING CAR

Oaklands were built in Pontiac, Michigan by the Oakland Buggy Company, which merged with General Motors. Dad's 6-60 model was first produced in 1913 and sold for $2,500 at the time. It had the steering wheel on the right, English style! In later years, the Oakland name was changed to Pontiac. This snapshot shows the car decorated with flowers for some holiday parade. On the 4th of July, we decorated it with flags and banners. Independence Day was always a big celebration in Olivia with GAR veterans from the Civil War and maybe some from the Renville Rangers, which was a citizens' militia that had been organized to protect the frontier from the Sioux. We always looked forward to the band music, patriotic speeches and fireworks at dusk. Our family usually drove a few miles north to our "shack" on Lake Kandiyohi for a fish supper and our own roman candles and sparklers in the evening.

THE BUICK CAREENS BACKWARDS

Later that first morning, barely 70-miles or so from home, the Windhorsts had a frightening near-accident that made them want to turn around, head for home and forget about the Yellowstone Trail. As told by Kathleen, it was the Empeys who first noticed that there might be trouble.

"James," the usually jolly Mrs. Empey addressed her husband, "I can see the Dowlings back there, but I can't see the Windhorsts."

Empeys, in their Ford, had chugged up the hill outside Appleton, Minnesota, and for once the engine had not over-heated and Jim had not stopped to pour water into the radiator from the canvas bag hung on the side of the car. The cars were all thirsty in 1913. In the vanguard, Jim, a large and jolly man, already versed in the ways of cars, curbed his enthusiasm and brought their vehicle to a stop. No need to pull off onto the shoulder, even had there been one. In all the miles of Minnesota rolling prairie, their cars were the only ones. M.J. Dowling drove alongside in his touring Oakland, with his wife in her duster and large veiled hat, primly beside him, the three girls bouncing along on the back seat.

A frightening near accident on first day of trip leaves drivers shaken!

"Why the halt?" Dowling asked as soon as he had really stopped the car. The day was fine, hot and dusty, so that the curtains were unsnapped and rolled up neatly. The girls called out, "Where are the Windhorsts?"

After a few minutes of discussion, both cars turned around and headed back east. They drove down the hill and stopped at its foot, where the Windhorst Buick sat.

The Windhorst son, their driver, looked nonplussed. He said he had tried to get up the hill, but could not! His father and mother and three sisters were standing nearby, apparently terrified of what might happen. Twice, they had tried to get up the hill and twice careened back down. The second time they all scrambled out of the car and were tearfully saying they wished they were home again, back there in Olivia, Minnesota, and why had they ever left? It was Mr. Dowling's fault. He had persuaded the men to go along with him on the Yellowstone Trail to blaze a new frontier and the women had thought it would be fun to see the park and to ride around in a big coach with four horses once they were there. And now they could not get up a hill and would probably tip over and all be killed if they tried.

The four men went into a huddle and finally made up their minds to try something different. "Boss" as the Windhorst son was known, would get in the car, turn it around and BACK UP the hill. Fearfully, all watched. After many starts, a white-faced Boss got up the hill and backed well beyond it. The family was given a ride in the Oakland to join him. All got into their Buick, somewhat fearfully, and the three cars started again on their trek west.

Until, that is, the Buick had to stop again, just 20-miles down the road with the first flat tire of the trip. As one person remarked, "Some days, there'll be months like that!" In that summer of 1913, traveling by auto was certainly novel and not all pleasure!

SOMEDAY.... A GREAT HIGHWAY!

In 1913, there were very few good roads. The Twin Cities-Aberdeen-Yellowstone Park Trail Association was a private group working to create a

great highway across the northern states. Joe Parmley was the founder of the trail and a friend of Dad's. He had mapped a proposed route, but nobody had yet driven the complete distance from Minneapolis to Yellowstone Park. Here was an opportunity for Michael Dowling, "the mechanized man" to score another first.

In those days we had no gravel roads, or just a smattering of them, so that we never knew what we might run into. The country graders ran a windrow of sod into the center of the road, but cars were built high enough to straddle most of them. Otherwise, it was a question of keeping the car on the side without slipping into the ditch. Roads were narrow, and usually of black dirt that could be disastrous when wet. The car simply slid in every direction except where you wanted it to go. So we tried to drive when rain was not imminent. Roads took a long time to dry and had mud holes that made us wonder if we could pull through. Often, one of us had to walk ahead to test the bottom and see which way would be safest for the attempt to go. I took this picture of the Oakland, top up and windshield in place, somewhere in the Dakota badlands.

When it snowed, people stored their cars until spring. Dad took the battery out, drained the radiator, jacked up the wheels, covered the body and that's how the Oakland stayed all winter. Sleeping in the barn alongside our buggy, with our nine cats prowling around and lying on it and leaving paw prints on the hood, which Father didn't like at all!

HEADING WEST WITH DOWLING

Our little caravan to Yellowstone traveled very close together, so if one car stopped, the others stopped, too. When one driver had trouble, the others were there to help. Stops were often made to allow overheated engines time to cool. Water for the radiators was carried in canvas water bags. I took this picture to show our big touring car in the lead with the lighter and smaller Ford behind and the medium-size Buick bringing up the rear. All three cars had much higher clearance than today's automobiles and were better suited to off-road travel. But, the height of the seats above the ground made running boards a real necessity for climbing on-board. The Ford had its steering wheel on the left. There was no standard design at the time, so it was up to the car company where they put it.

A BAD BRIDGE IN THE DAKOTAS

It was one thing to draw a line on a map and rally boosters along the route, but to actually create a trans-continental highway without state or federal money presented a huge challenge. In 1913, less than 1-percent of voters paid any federal income tax. One's poll tax could be paid in cash or by showing up with shovel in hand to donate labor on the town or country roads. I took this snapshot to show us following the route of the Yellowstone Trail along a farm section line. Everyone is watching the Windhorst Buick as it comes around a partially collapsed wooden bridge and fords a stream.

WE CROSS THE MISSOURI BY FERRY

Mobridge, SD was named for the Missouri River and Milwaukee Railroad Bridge in the background. But, in 1913, there was still no bridge across the river for automobiles. So, we crossed on the ferry boat "Carolina." The toll was $1.00 for each car and driver and the crossing took two trips. The larger, heavier Oakland was brought over first and the other two cars came together on the second trip. This is my picture of the Oakland ready to land. Only 700 cars crossed the river by ferry that whole year.

We filled our gasoline tanks before leaving Mobridge to cross the Indian Reservation. There weren't any filling stations. Gasoline was mostly sold at general stores or automobile repair garages. It was usually drained from barrels into 5-gallon measuring cans and then into the car. A few places had "Bowser" self-measuring pumps that could feed gasoline directly into the cars. Those pumps were operated by hand.

IF LOST, PUT ON A SMILE!

There was no road through the Standing Rock Indian Reservation. The Indians had never built one across their vast acres of land. Nor, was there anything in sight on those open plains which might help to show the way. A dim trace of horse and wagon tracks seemed to meander along, but eventually disappeared in the grass and dust. When he could no longer see a trail, Father brought our car to a stop. "Now, where in heaven are we?" he asked in a cheerful Irish brogue. "Somebody, please get out and find us a road."

As a boy, Dad had spent 3-summers alone on the open range watching over a herd of 500 cattle. He had lived close to nature, camped under the stars and always found his way. But, now he was lost on the prairie near where Chief Sitting Bull had once had his camp. As our party of "trail blazers" stopped to study the maps, an Indian man appeared on horseback. I wondered if he had been trailing us? He rode twice around our cars, looking us over, and then pulled his painted pony to a stop by Dad. The Indian pretended not to speak English as Father started pointing around and shouting "McLaughlin? McLaughlin?" It was like a wild west adventure story, but finally the Indian got the idea and led us all around in circles, before bringing us over a hill and into McLaughlin, SD. I had been getting a bit worried about running out of gasoline and was glad when the buildings of town came into view.

My father was a man without hands or feet, who had experienced many close calls and narrow escapes and always come out smiling. He told people that his handicap was God's greatest blessing because he began to think, to work and to win as he had never done before. He had incredible courage and determination, a quick Irish wit and charm. He believed fervently in the value of education and hard work. He never waited for good luck to come his way. He went after it. When he put on his "legs" each morning, he also put on his smile!

ROLLING DOWN A BUMPY TRAIL

All counties and rural townships had networks of farm roads or trails that often led nowhere. There was no main highway across the northern states. One county in North Dakota boasted that its roads were so good (and flat) that drivers could drive the whole way across it in high gear. In other places, drivers had to shift down a gear or two in order to pass over rocky outcrops or get through streams. There were also obstacles like bridges collapsed or fence gates to be opened and no clear trail ahead. I took this snapshot at a narrow cut between two hilly buttes on the way out of the badlands. Many farmers looked upon automobiles as playthings of the wealthy and were against raising taxes to build better roads. In 1913, most tourists and travelers still went any long distance by rail.

A PUNCTURE ON THE PRAIRIE

The first part of our trip was not very scenic and the long summer days were uncomfortably hot. This is my photograph of the Windhorst family fixing a puncture that happened, somehow, way out in the middle of nowhere while marking a new trail across flat, open prairie near Bowman, ND. That family always seemed to be having bad luck with their Buick. Whenever we came to a particularly steep hill, most of them had to get out, lighten the load and walk. Sometimes, one of them rode with us.

FORDING THE LITTLE MISSOURI

All three autos had to ford the Little Missouri River at Marmarth, ND. I looked back from our car to take this shot of the Windhorst Buick in the water. We also had to ford across many smaller streams and once a car got stuck in the middle and everybody helped get it across and out. Crossing any river was a bit of a risk, but more so with muddy water and a flowing current. Sometimes, there were marker stakes warning of quick-sand. Having learned by experience, Dad hired a "pilot" to lead us across the Powder River when we came to it. Our guide told us that river was a "mile wide and an inch deep, too wet to plow and too thick to drink." He took us on quite a detour to a place upstream, where there was a good, solid bottom and we all made it across safely.

STALLED BY HERDS OF SHEEP

Herds of sheep sometimes forced us to stop and wait until the trail ahead was clear. I took this photo as we were approaching Miles City, near Knowlton, Montana. Much of the West was still "open range" for sheep and cattle. And, directions were often confusing on the maps we used. Our maps would say things like "at the next big tree turn right, pass a school house, farm buildings 5-miles ahead, follow small stream for half a mile" and so forth. One person had to be watching the map at all times to keep everybody on the right track.

WAGONBOX LUNCH AT THE MIZPAH RANCH

We found shade and water and enjoyed lunch one day in the yard of the Mizpah Ranch in Montana. Here, my sister Kay saw horses, lariats, stuffed animal trophies, corrals, homemade fence posts and lots of cowboy and western things. During rest periods like this, we could rearrange our luggage, take a walk, study the map and relax. We were all tired, hot, hungry and cross, but, rest and food perked us up. During one such break, we girls almost stepped on a rattlesnake as we wandered about.

Another time, we stopped at a little country store with a well and pump in the side yard. The Windhorst sisters spread out their picnic on the shady front porch of the store. But, we all had to pick up and move when customers arrived and walked in and out the door. We hadn't realized the store was open for business.

MOTHER WAS "BOSS OF THE BUNCH! SHE HAD OUR LUNCH!"

Shady places for the cars to stop were sometimes few and far between. Mother would see a nice place, but by the time she said so, the car was beyond it and Dad would decide to keep on driving. She never complained, even when we had a puncture or were stuck in mud or lost the trail. If she was exasperated, the most she would do was say, "Oh, ginger!" Mother was blue eyed, energetic and very Norwegian. She had worked as assistant editor for a newspaper before she was married. On the trail, she watched over us girls, took care of the luggage, sewing and first aid kits and, most importantly, our lunches! It was always a treat to open her filled to over-flowing picnic basket and discover what she had put inside. The basket would have been prepared each morning at our hotel or stopping place and was sure to have both white and dark bread and lots of tasty fixings for open face sandwiches. She liked cucumber pickles and had brought along a big box of oranges and apples on the running board. She would also have some yummy candies or cookies for dessert. There was a small ice chest to keep some things cool, but ice was not always available where we stayed. Mother helped keep everyone amused with riddles to guess, songs to sing and "Spy the White Horse" or other games to play. If something struck her funny, she would giggle and laugh and giggle some more until the tears came. She always believed that you find happiness by creating happiness in others. Jennie Dowling was the kind of person who liked a challenge and I believed that she could do anything! In later years, she was a founder of Camp Courage, a nationally recognized program for the disabled and handicapped.

NOT EXACTLY GRAVEL

Miles City was our first stopping place after we got to Montana. The road from there was good, but the so-called gravel included many large size stones and made for a bumpy ride. However, our Oakland had plenty of clearance to drive the trail without hitting a rock, anywhere. Dad told a reporter that the need was not so much to improve the trail, but to place signs making it easier to follow. Furthermore, he predicted a "Golden Stream" of tourists would someday drive it. All of this when only about 20 people in Olivia even owned cars!

#

#   #

At Pompey's Pillar, we saw the sandstone outcropping where William Clark carved his name in 1806. There were other initials carved there too, but I doubt if anybody in our "bunch" left a mark. Dad and Mother very strongly disapproved of any graffiti or writing one's name in public places.

#

#   #

We stayed the next night at Billings, where we found a way to get to a porch near the roof of our hotel. From there, we saw the country around about with the twinkling lights of the city at our feet. There were some cliffs called the Rim Rocks.

DOWN A 20-PERCENT GRADE

Just east of Columbus, MT, we encountered a steep 20-percent grade. Dad put the car in low gear and cautiously led the way down. The car had an instrument like a carpenter's level that showed how steep the hills. That hill would have been dangerous for any car without good, safe steering and brakes.

Columbus was a pleasant village in the foothills of the mountains by the Yellowstone River. I think we stayed there overnight. Rates at commercial hotels averaged $1.00 a day plus meals. Most were 2-story wood or brick buildings located near the railroad depot. The usual guests were traveling salesmen or engineers and brakemen from the trains. There was perhaps a small dining room in the hotel, or a café close by. Rooms on the upper floor had a coil of rope in a corner so guests could escape out a window in case of fire. I always wondered if I might discover bedbugs in the room.

One night, the Windhorst sisters were put in a room that was already rented to a man who happened to be out of town for the night. There was no key for the room, so the girls pushed a heavy dresser in front of the door.

A PUNCTURE ON BENSON'S BLUFF

Changing a flat tire on a steep mountain grade was difficult because it was hard to find a level place to put the jack. The car would tilt and roll off unless rocks were used to hold it. Here, the men are replacing a tire on the Oakland while it is headed down a mountain road. I snapped this picture from below the guardrail along a narrow pass on Benson's Bluff just to show the big boulders and rocky terrain. Roads in some parts of Montana were built by convicts.

COOLING ENGINES ON BENSON'S BLUFF

I took this photo of the three cars stopped to cool their engines on a
mountain road over Benson's Bluff near Springdale.

YELLOWSTONE RIVER FROM BENSON'S BLUFF

We were high above the Yellowstone River when I snapped this scenic
photograph of the river below and mountains in the distance.

A GOOD TOURIST ROAD!

The cost of building roads across Montana was very expensive per mile because of the many streams to be bridged and cuts that had to be made through solid rock. I took this photograph near Springdale, Montana where we were driving along the Yellowstone River in single file with a vertical rock face on one side and a steep drop-off on the other. Roads like this had to be blasted out with dynamite. They always had a good surface of gravel, but falling rocks could present an obstacle.

NEAR HUNTER'S HOT SPRINGS

The South Trail from Springdale to Livingston, Montana was a narrow, single track rock road with a wooden guard rail made of logs. It hugged the side of the mountain above the tracks of the Northern Pacific Railway and followed the course of the wild and scenic Yellowstone River. We crossed many mountain streams which rushed down through culverts. For some reason, we were advised to choose this better route and drive south of the river. It was in this vicinity that we caught our first real glimpse of the Rockies. It's hard to imagine that this road is now U.S. Interstate 94, a 4-lane, 65-mph freeway!

MICHAEL DANCED A JIG

Dad liked to stop in towns along the way to visit the offices of newspapers, tell reporters about our trip and get publicity for extending the Yellowstone Trail.

He would often roll up his trousers to show his wooden legs, stamp his "feet", kick about and dance a little Irish jig. This is a picture of him that was published in the Ladies' Home Journal magazine a few years after that Yellowstone trip. Dad told reporters, "If a man like I am with neither hands nor feet, can make this trip in a six cylinder car, underslung, and drive all the way myself with my wife and three children, and not have any accident, do all the repairing myself and all the driving, I do not see why any person who can drive a car can not make this grand trip." However, it took us 10-days to drive there instead of the 7-days he originally predicted. And it wasn't always a comfortable ride by any means. But, Dad could make it sound like a wonderous journey and I guess it really was!

We knew that automobiles were banned from Yellowstone, so we left the cars at Livingston, took a train to Gardiner and climbed aboard a coach to tour the park.

The Daily Enterprise.

OL. III, No. 255 — LIVINGSTON, MONTANA, WEDNESDAY, JULY 16, 1913

First Party to Complete Trip Over the Park Trail Arrives, With Speedometer Registering 999.1

Tuesday evening the first party to complete the trip over the new Yellowstone Park Trail, (designated as the Twin Cities-Aberdeen-Yellowstone Park Trail) arrived here after spending Tuesday at Hunters. The party arrived in Billings Monday afternoon as mentioned exclusively, in the Enterprise yesterday, and drive there spent Tuesday at Hunters and arrived here last night, leaving this morning on the Park branch train for Gardiner and will leave for a tour of Yellowstone National Park.

When the party arrived in Livingston, with their three autos, the speedometers registered 999.1 miles. They started from Olivia, Minn., which is 1014 miles west of St. Anthony Falls, making the total distance from the Twin Cities to Livingston practically 1100 miles over the Trail.

The party came in three different cars, they being a Ford, 1912 model; an Oakland, six cylinder, air horse power, underslung, with 126 inch wheel base, and a model 39 Buick, 1911 car.

In speaking to the Enterprise about the trip, M. J. Dowling, who is one of Minnesota's most enthusiastic good roads boosters and has been a speaker after of the Minnesota house of representatives for the last two terms, said "The lives for the last two terms, said "If two Sunday and have enjoyed every nor feet, can make this trip in a six cylinder car, underslung, and drive all the way myself with my wife, and three children, and not have any accident, but do all the driving, I do not see why any person who can drive a car can not make this grand trip." And Mr. Dowling is not speaking in a jesting manner when he speaks of himself as a man with neither hands nor feet for both hands are badly crippled, with no fingers on either hand. Mr. and Mrs. James Kenney of Olivia are taking this trip for their honeymoon tour although they have been married 25 years, but they had always postponed their honeymoon journey until now and are having the real time of their life.

All the men in the party were so impressed with the great good the trail will do for Montana cities and especially for Livingston, the terminus of the trail. They said people along the route did not realize to any extent whatsoever the great benefit the road would be to the country in general. If these three cars with 13 persons came over the route from one little town in Minnesota, think what will mean when people not only from Minnesota but from states all over the union and especially wealthy people from New York and Boston commence to use the trail.

And they find the expenses very reasonable along the journey.

The party consists of Mr. and Mrs. Dorothy, Marjorie and Kathleen, and Mrs. Wm. Windilos and children, Misses Ida, Leonora, Elsie and son, Oscar, and Mr. and Mrs. Jas. Kenney.

999.1 MILES TO LIVINGSTON, MONTANA

SEEING THE PARK BY STAGE COACH

A complete circle of the park took 5-days and Dad booked a special coach or surrey for our bunch to make the tour. We girls all wanted to ride up on the box with the driver and watch him handle the reins of the 4-horse team. Rules for the stage drivers were quite strict. They were not allowed to smoke on duty or leave the box while passengers were in the coach. And, they could never surrender the reins to any passengers. Drivers had to stay on schedule and keep at least 100-yards distance from the coach ahead. In those days, Yellowstone Park was governed by the U.S. Army, but in fact, operated mostly by concessionaires controlled by railroad interests. It wasn't until two years later that rules were changed and automobiles allowed to enter the park. And, it was another year after that before the National Park Service came into being and assumed the management of the park.

BILL PALMER, COACHMAN AND GUIDE

We had the same coach and driver for all of our tour. He kept us entertained with interesting stories about the history of the park, which was established as the first national park in America in 1872. He pointed out Osprey-eagles and told us

about the animals, trees, flowers and formations such as the mountain of glass and various hot springs and pools. He told me that if I tossed my handkerchief into one of the geysers, it would come out miles away, washed and clean! He also told tall tales about the "Wild West", encounters with grizzly bears, mountain lions, Indians and prospectors. In this picture, you can see Mrs. Empey and Dad inside the coach and one of the girls is barely visible up on the box.

Old Faithful Geyser

Mammoth Hot Springs Hotel & Fort Yellowstone from Jupiter Terrace 1913

RELAXING AT OLD FAITHFUL INN

As we circled Yellowstone on the "grand loop" we stayed overnight at each of the Park's great, luxury hotels. It was exciting for us to be shown to our own room, to be given ice water and to have the shades adjusted and the beds turned down. There was pleasure in having the head waiter be solicitous about serving a steak cooked the way Dad preferred. That was usually "rare and sliced" as he liked to tell people, "I am an omnivorous reader, but a carnivorous eater." And, he would send his plate back to the kitchen if he wasn't satisfied. I especially liked it when they brought a dessert cart to our table, after the meal, so Mother could choose just the kind of pastry she desired.

I was quite impressed by the New Canyon Hotel which I found very attractive and more modern than the rest. It had an art and souvenir shop and an orchestra which played concerts every afternoon and in the evening with dancing afterwards. I was told that one could walk a mile, just going around the grounds!

But, Old Faithful Inn was my real favorite because it was built of logs and seemed more mountain rustic, with its great stone fireplace and big, open lobby. It was also close to Old Faithful geyser. In this snapshot Kathleen is sitting on the porch of the second balcony at the Inn.

The Lake Hotel looked out on Yellowstone Lake, where one could fish or arrange a ride on a steam powered launch. The Mammoth Hotel was near Fort Yellowstone and the other hotel was the Fountain Hotel. All were built to serve wealthy travelers who could afford to come from eastern cities by rail. Automobiles and new roads would soon make the nation's park accessible to every family, rich and poor alike.

BERNARD MAMER
DRUGGIST
OLIVIA   **MINNESOTA**

R No. .... Date ....

Address ....

Alcohol   4 oz

Sweet oil   2 oz

Turpentine oil - 1/4 oz

Organum   1 oz

Camphor Gum   1. oz

aq Ammnia   1/4 oz

Chloroform   1/2 oz

S.
    Liniment.   386494
For external use only.
                                            M. D.

WRE

FEEDING THE YELLOWSTONE BEARS

Bears of the park were a popular tourist attraction. Some people foolishly fed them apples. I snapped this close-up photo from behind a soldier's back when several of the guests ventured out one evening to see the bears at the garbage piles behind the hotel. The man in the background, wearing a clerical collar, was Father Paul Reinfels from Paloma, Illinois. I thought he resembled a bear. Later, I bought three carved wooden bears as souvenirs.

Back in the privacy of his hotel room, my father removed his wooden legs and prowled around the floor on his elbows and knees like a bear while playing a game of hide and seek with my little sister Kay. Then, Mother massaged his stumps with his own, very special liniment concocted by Bernard Mamer's drugstore back home in Olivia. Its prescription formula included alcohol, turpentine, chloroform, ammonia and other oils and extracts to relieve his aches and sores.

Dad also found time for a long, relaxing soak and perhaps a mud bath at one of the pools or hot springs. He and Mother had been mud bathing for years at a health spa near Shakopee, Minnesota. But, I never liked the mud or sulfur smells.

YELLOWSTONE "BUNCH" DRESSED FOR THE TRAIL

All of the cars were open touring models with leatherette or fabric tops and side curtains flapping in the breeze. So, drivers and passengers dressed appropriately. Women and girls usually wore dusters, hats and scarves. Dad liked

to wear gauntlets and goggles.

Dad had fun telling newspapers and people we met that Mr. and Mrs. Empey were "just married." I think they had actually been married for maybe 35 years, but never taken a honeymoon. Anyway, Dad thought it made for a good story and people sometimes believed it because of the way she looked and dressed with her wide hat and scarf tied around it.

When a reporter asked Dad if "13" in the party had brought bad luck, he answered that the "Hoodoo" hadn't haunted us at all except for a few punctures and a fan belt on the Ford that was easily repaired. I gave my Kodak to our stage driver to take this photo at Emerald Pool in the park.

FINDING SHELTER IN A RAINSTORM

We were on our way home and somewhere east of Great Falls, around Floweree, Montana, when it started to rain. During one particularly heavy cloudburst, we were forced to snap on the side curtains and head for any shelter we could find. Dad could hardly see to steer because we had only one windshield wiper and that had to be worked by hand. Luckily, we came to a solitary farmstead that was occupied by a family named Trackwell. They welcomed our crowd in from the downpour and invited us to sleep overnight, on the floor or anyplace we could find a spot. Kathleen said it was like camping out!

Next morning, the Trackwells prepared a big, ranch-style breakfast for everybody. We had a contest to see who could eat the most pancakes. Their hospitality was very much appreciated. Dad said those farmers and ranchers were "the real west"!

ROSEMARY'S RIDE

Father had promised the Trackwell's daughter, Rosemary, a ride in the Oakland. So, after breakfast, Dad and that family went for a short spin down the trail to see if the sunshine had dried it out enough for travel. I took this photograph of Rosemary right after her exciting automobile ride. I think she wore ear muffs to keep the wind out of her ears! Rosemary had been to the fair in Bozeman and seen automobiles around Great Falls, but never one so grand and powerful as our big, new, Oakland touring car that was able to go almost a mile-a-minute on a straight and level road. Rosemary was about my age, enjoyed talking about roping and riding contests and was fascinated to hear about the cyclone shelter in our cellar at home and about Olivia's girl basketball team. I believe the Trackwells may have been sheep farmers. Rosemary was used to chores and taking care of animals.

STUCK FOR AN HOUR ON A GUMBO FLAT

Although the trail seemed dry near Trackwell's, we soon encountered wet and slippery muck where the car skidded all around, even with chains on both front and rear wheels. It wasn't long before we became stalled for an hour on a muddy, gumbo flat. I think Marjorie took this snapshot of our big, heavy Oakland bogged down in mud and me, with shoes and stockings off, trying to fill the ruts with grass or weeds for traction. I was afraid we might have to find a farmer with a team of horses to pull us out, until Mr. Empey came along and somehow managed to tighten the chains on the wheels and get us moving. Then, it was "all aboard" again and let's keep rolling.

PAST AN INDIAN VILLAGE

Dad drove a different route home, along the Great Northern Railroad. I took no pictures of the country between Bozeman and Fort Peck, but we must have gone through Helena, Great Falls and Havre. It's all so long ago I can't remember. Maybe I was low on film. However, I did snap this photograph of Teepees on the Fort Peck Indian Reservation in Montana. Only a few children came out to watch our automobiles parade by. No adults showed their faces. If you look closely, you can see slabs of meat that were hung to dry in the sun.

A couple of hours after I took this picture, the Windhorsts' Buick broke down and this time had to be left at Williston, ND. Unable to complete the return trip from Yellowstone, the unlucky Windhorsts returned home to Olivia by rail.

A LEARNING EXPERIENCE!

Our new Oakland made it all the way to Yellowstone without mechanical trouble, but we had a major blowout near Devils Lake, ND on the way home. This time, I took a picture of Mr. Empey on his hands and knees changing the tire as Dad and others look on. The Oakland had demountable rims and we carried two spare tires.

But, the car had to be jacked up, and if repairable, the tire and rubber inner tube removed, the tube patched by hand, reinserted in the casing and then re-inflated using a hand air pump and remounted on the rim and wheel. I watched and was told I must be able to do all of this alone before Dad would let me drive. No wonder that Mother never learned to drive!

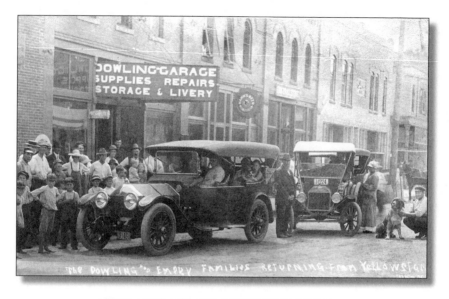

THE "TRAIL BLAZERS" RETURN

On August 5, 1913, at about 2:00 pm, we finished our last day's run from Glenwood, Minnesota, drove into Olivia, paraded down Main Street past a line of horses and wagons tethered to hitching posts and rolled to a stop in front of Dad's garage which was next to the bank. As Dad and Mr. Empey shut down their engines, we were surrounded by a little crowd of townspeople on hand to welcome us home. When asked if I had seen any Indians, I told about getting lost near the stronghold of Chief Sitting Bull and about some of our other adventures. All of us were peppered with questions about the performance of the cars and conditions along the way. A few days later, in the Twin Cities, the entire membership of the Minneapolis Automobile Club turned out to welcome my father and acclaim his party as "the first to drive the complete distance from Minneapolis to Yellowstone and return by automobile."

I don't know who took this photograph, but the man at far right, with cap and pipe and kneeling with a dog, is probably Mother's brother Harald T. Bordewich who was married to Flora Windhorst. He worked for Dad at the bank and was a representative for the Yellowstone Trail Association in Olivia.

The 1913 Yellowstone Trail Blazers
"First to Drive the Trail"

MICHAEL J. DOWLING-
1913 Oakland
7 passenger 6/60

Mayor of Olivia, Minnesota
President, Olivia State Bank
Director, Yellowstone Trail Association

Mrs. Jennie Bordewich Dowling
Children: Dorothy
                    Marjorie
                    Kathleen

WILLIAM WINDHORST-
1911 Buick
Model 39

Owner of Lumberyard, Olivia, Minnesota

Mrs. William Windhorst (Mary)
Children: Ida
                    Leonora
                    Elsie
                    Oscar ("Boss")

JAMES EMPEY-
1912 Ford
Model T

Manager of Farmers Elevator,
Olivia, Minnesota

Mrs. James Empey (Lil)

Minneapolis-St. Paul To Yellowstone National Park

MINNESOTA

Minneapolis/St. Paul
Hopkins
Excelsior
Waconia
Young America
Norwood
Plato
Glencoe
Sumter
Brownton
Syewary
Buffalo Lake
Hector
Bird Island

OLIVIA
Danube
Renville
Sacred Heart
Granite Falls
Wegdahl P.O.
Montevideo
Watson
Milan
Appleton
Correll
Odessa
Ortonville

SOUTH DAKOTA
Big Stone City
Milbank
Twin Brooks
Marvin
Summit
Waubay
***Webster
Holmquist
Bristol
Andover
Groten
James
Aberdeen

SOUTH DAKOTA (Cont.)

Craven
***Ipswich
Beebe
Roscoe
Gretna
Bowdle
Java
Selby
Sitka
Glenham
Mobridge
Wakpala
Mahto
McLaughlin
Tatanka
***McIntosh
Watouga
Morristown
Keldron
Thunder Hawk
Lemmon
Petrel ND
White Butte

NORTH DAKOTA
Haynes
Hettinger
Bucyrus
Reeder
Gascoyne
Scranton
***Bowman
Griffin
Rhame
Marmarth
Montline

MONTANA
Baker
Tonquin
Plevna
Westmore
***Ismay

MONTANA (Cont.)

Mildred
Fallon
Terry
Blanchford
Zero
Shirley
Tusler
***Miles City
Paragon
Calabar
Thurlow
Cartersville
Forsyth
Howard
Finch
McCormicks Seed Ranch
Sanders
Hysham
Myers
Junction
Custer
Bull Mt.
Pompey's Piller
Newton
Huntley
***Billings
Foster Sta.
Laurel
Park City
Rapids
Columbus
Reed Point
Grey Cliff
Big Timber
***Hunter Hot Springs
Springdale P.O.
***Livingston
Lime Spur
Emigrant
Dailey
Miner
Sphynx
Corwin Hot Springs
Electric
Gardiner

NOTE: It is unclear whether the Dowling party left their cars outside the Park at Livingston or at Gardiner? Dorothy told it both ways, but a contemporary newspaper account said they would leave the cars at Livingston.

Because of road and weather delays, the trip took about 10-days instead of Dowling's originally predicted 7-days. The return took 15 days over a different route. In all, the party drove a distance of about 2,500 miles. *** Known overnight stops.

Route of the Yellowstone Trail

Minnesota

Minneapolis & St. Paul

Olivia

North Dakota

South Dakota

Aberdeen

Mobridge

Marmarth

Missouri River

Miles City

Billings

Montana

Livingston

Yellowstone Park

Wyoming

YELLOWSTONE • TRAIL

Distance: Olivia to Livingston
999.1 miles

1914

EAST TO PLYMOUTH ROCK

1914

MAPPING THE TRAIL EAST

We all knew that Dad loved to travel, so I wasn't surprised when he started talking the next year about taking the whole family for another "grand summer trip!"

But, nobody expected it to be a wondrous voyage by steamship. "It won't be like the time the President sent me to the Philippines in advance of the Taft Commission." Dad promised. "That Army troop transport was nothing but a converted cattle boat. This summer, we'll be sailing aboard a fine, big passenger ship with comfortable staterooms, a promenade deck, several cozy parlors, a music room, a writing room and a lovely main dining saloon with white table cloths and crystal water glasses. You girls will meet the Captain, have the run of the ship and enjoy a glorious time."

Now, Marjorie and I were becoming excited.

> *"The roads out east are all good roads"*

"Papa! Is it an ocean liner?"

"Where are we going? Papa, where?"

"You're not taking us to Norway?" Mother asked.

"The name of the ship is the SS Tionesta and it will be taking us toward my old home in the Berkshires, where I was born poor, but Irish!" Dad declared. "I've discovered that we can drive up to Duluth, load the Oakland right aboard ship with us and cruise down the Great Lakes to Buffalo. That will greatly shorten the run and let us enjoy a nice, leisurely drive across New York State to Massachusetts."

"So, this is really about the Yellowstone Trail, again," Hattie decided.

"That and a pleasure trip," Dad admitted. "Somebody needs to begin mapping the eastern end of the Trail and find sponsors now because those Lincoln Highway people are working hard on their coast-to-coast route and have already claimed New York City. We need to win Boston and Plymouth for our great highway."

"And, you're just Irish enough to do it," Hattie agreed.

"This trip won't be all about the Trail," Dad went on. "We'll have lots of time to sight-see through the beautiful Berkshire Hills and be visiting my aunts and uncles and cousins by the dozens."

Mother still looked perplexed. "The Windhorsts and Empeys haven't mentioned anything about this."

"Those folks have other plans," Dad replied. "So, it will be just our family, this year. But, won't we be motoring in style on a grand, patriotic loop through Boston with all of its historic landmarks and then down to Plymouth Rock where the Pilgrims landed and back to Boston to follow the ride of Paul Revere?"

"Er veien velskapt?" Gram Bordewich ventured to ask. "Are the roads well made? I mean well built?" She thought Dad was King and loved riding with him on drives through the countryside. But, she didn't like splattering through mud holes or jouncing over bumps.

Dad reached over, smiled and patted her shoulder gently with his one remaining part of a hand. (His fist without fingers). "The roads out East are all good roads. We'll be on the Post Road all the way from Albany to Boston. It's not like the open range or endless prairies we traveled out West."

"But, what if we break down, like the Windhorsts did last year?" Mother wanted to know.

"I'm optimistic that will never happen," Dad enthused. "If it does, we'll never be far from some city or town with mechanics available. But, the Oakland is a fine, dependable car. I'll wager that Dorothy and Marjorie are the only mechanics I'll ever need."

The Oakland was running smoothly and well maintained by the mechanics at Dowling's Garage. Also, Dad had just purchased two new tires. Still, I worried a little and wished I could be as optimistic as he was.

"When do you want to leave?" Mother finally asked.

"Let's be on our way July 21st. That's a Tuesday. I have a meeting the night before, but nothing on my calendar after that except an August meeting of the Trail Association about some roads out West. I can easily skip that."

Dad was Mayor of Olivia and very active in politics as well as business. It was a pleasure when he could get away.

His blue eyes glanced around the dining table at each of us. "Hattie and Harald will run the bank again," he said. "And Gram will be just fine here. We'll have weeks of fun on the trip and you, my dearest daughters, will come back filled with energy, in time to start school again. In the meantime, you will have learned more about this great land of ours than if you spent a whole year in a classroom reading books."

How well I remember that last, hectic weekend before we left. I took

Sunday breakfast upstairs to Dad, who was in bed. Mother and Father's bedroom was at the head of the stairs on the second floor. Dad liked to stay in bed all morning and read his Sunday papers undisturbed. It was a burden for him to wear his wooden legs all week, so he needed a day of relaxation. The rest of us kept busy and spent most of those last days packing for the trip.

Then, on July 21st, we were off for an unforgettable summer during which I had many new experiences, saw the Atlantic Ocean for the first time and traveled some 5,000 miles before returning home to Olivia.

A REST STOP NEAR DULUTH

I took this photograph on the first day of our trip when we stopped at Fond du Lac, which is just a little west of Duluth. It may have been on an Indian Reservation. Dad was very interested in the history of Minnesota and the early explorers and fur trade. He said this was once the site of a Hudson Bay Company trading post. But, I don't think there was anything left to see.

It was always a pleasure to stop, get out of the car and walk around for awhile. When those old engines got hot, you could just smell the fumes coming up through the floorboards and dash. So, when anyone started feeling a bit nauseated, it was good to rest and breathe some fresh air.

Dad had a collection of different walking canes which he kept in a brass umbrella stand by our front door. I think he carried his "Irish Shillelagh" on this trip. But, I'm not sure if you can see it in the picture.

UNDERWAY ON LAKE SUPERIOR

We had rooms overnight at a hotel in Duluth. There was a Black Bear mounted upright on its hind legs on display in the lobby. It appeared very lifelike and fascinating. Bears were often sighted wandering into that city.

After a good breakfast, we drove down a steep hill to the harbor and found our ship. We watched as the Oakland was hoisted aboard. I think ours was the only car carried on that voyage. But, freight of all kinds was taken aboard. Many passengers traveled with trunks, foot lockers, boxes and bags, dogs and pets. Lots of furniture, crates and barrels were also being shipped.

When all was ready, the ship blew its whistle, which was very loud, and we were underway. We all stood by the rail to watch as we steamed out beneath the famous aerial lift bridge which stands above that harbor like a landmark. Kathleen climbed into the rigging. She said to be a lookout and get a better view. But, there was only an occasional ore boat and the waves to see.

ABOARD THE SS TIONESTA

Mackinac Island.

The steamship SS Tionesta was built in 1903 and was operated on the Great Lakes by the Anchor Line, a subsidiary of the Pennsylvania Railroad. It could carry up to 350 passengers as well as freight and automobiles. There was a single funnel or smokestack aft.

It was a five day trip and like an ocean voyage, because we were out of sight of land for so long. We found it fascinating to go through the locks at Sault Ste. Marie. The boat was ocean size, comfortable with good meals, games in progress and lots of sunshine and fresh air. Considering prices now, I don't think the freight for the car was too much.

The ship docked at Mackinac Island in Lake Huron to let all of the passengers go ashore and sightsee. There were no cars allowed, but we took a buggy ride around the island and saw the Sugar Loaf Cave, Arch Rock, Point Lookout and other places of interest.

This snapshot shows the SS Tionesta docked at the island. We did lots of chasing around the decks and I posed Kathleen for pictures in the rigging, capping the capstan and forward near the bow. Dad was right about us having the run of the ship!

After Mackinac, it was all water until we entered the river near Detroit and saw the big homes and yachts around Lake St. Clair.

HOW COMFORTABLE WAS IT?

Dad could be very persuasive and charming. When people in New York and Massachusetts asked about his first, trail-blazing adventure trip

through the "wild west" to Yellowstone, he smiled and answered that it was a comfortable trip and one that any family could take. "It was a pleasure to have my lovely wife along and my girls, Dorothy and Marjorie were my only mechanic and guide."

"Right now, the Trail begins at Minneapolis and continues only into Montana," he explained. "But, work on improving and extending the road is going ahead rapidly. Someday it will be a good road in both directions, to Plymouth Rock as well as to Puget Sound."

"It's not just a trail for Fords," he joked, but a road you can drive in a regular automobile. My Oakland came over the mountain crossings without touching a rock anywhere."

"We had a grand trip to Yellowstone," he asserted. "In fact, it was so comfortable that little Kathleen snoozed most of the way!" When he said that I knew he was talking blarney, because that wasn't how I remembered that awful trip, at all.

FROM BUFFALO TO SCHENECTADY

Our run across New York followed the existing post road (US-20) for most of the way, except when we took a sightseeing shortcut to Cooperstown. Our home in Olivia was overflowing with books, even in our "reading room" on the 3rd-floor. In fact, Dad had one of the best collections of books in the county. I loved to read stories by James Fenimore Cooper and wanted to see the countryside around Otsego Lake, which Cooper called "Glimmerglass" in his Leatherstocking Tales. This was once the edge of America's western frontier.

Dad thought it would be fun to see where the first game of baseball was played, in Cooperstown in 1839. He had once managed the Renville team and told us that "every rig in town, including the railroad hand car, pulled out to the ball game when we played at Granite Falls!"

We drove around Otsego Lake and then up through the Cherry Valley to Canajoharie, from where we followed the road east alongside the New York Central Railroad, the Erie Canal and the Mohawk River bluffs to Schenectady. Above is a picture I took of barges on the canal.

We stopped at a Quaker village to see their hand crafts and hear of their customs and visit their shops. We bought some maple sugar and Dad arranged for so many pounds of it to be shipped to him. It came in 10-pound pails and he sold it to his friends in Olivia. We ate gobs of it in syrup for pancakes and waffles and French toast and we made maple pralines from it.

A GOOD PLACE TO REST

There wasn't any traffic! We seldom met another car. And, if we did, they would always wave and often stop to chat. So, Dad felt free to stop anywhere on the roadway to get out, walk around, stretch and even have lunch without having to worry about blocking traffic.

I took this picture of the Oakland stopped under a telegraph pole at noon, somewhere in New York. "We'll have to take turns standing by the pole for shade." somebody said. "There's only enough shade for Kay, but she'll have to stand sideways. And not wave her arms or they'll get sunburned." Our antics gave Mother the giggles and pretty soon everybody was in a better mood and ready to go on.

On a fine road like this, Father could drive right along at 45-mph or so. The Oakland was big and easy to steer, but it had a really stiff clutch which made it hard to drive in stop-and-go parades. Dad got pleasure from driving and was always our treasurer. He said that when he got home he weighed more than when he left, but had considerable less money.

AN AUTOMOBILE ON FIRE

Early automobiles were not always safe or even very reliable. Some were "electrics", others were "steamers", but most ran on gasoline. Car engines sometimes over-heated, wires shorted and sparked, batteries exploded, fuel lines leaked and many cars had headlamps that were lit by acetylene gas. I snapped this picture of a car which had caught on fire somewhere along the road in New York State. A small crowd of onlookers stood by just watching it burn. Of course, there was no highway patrol or fire department to call for help and no way to telephone even if there had been.

DRIVING ALONG THE MOHAWK

This picture of the Oakland was taken between Canajoharie and Schenectady on a narrow, single lane road carved out of the Mohawk River bluffs. This stretch is now Interstate 90, but when we drove it in 1914, it was little more than a trail.

Most roads in New England were good gravel and well maintained. The rivers and streams were bridged. Local automobile clubs had put up all sorts of confusing trail signs to various destinations. It was usually best to inquire about road conditions ahead. Dad often stopped at local newspapers or banks to ask advice.

THE ROOFTOPS OF PITTSFIELD

We stayed overnight at the Kimball Hotel in the city of Pittsfield, Massachusetts. Marjorie, Kay and I explored all of the floors and hallways of the hotel and somehow discovered a stairway leading up to the roof, where we had an excellent view of the city in all directions. I captured this photograph of the downtown area with my Kodak Brownie camera. It shows double streetcar tracks, but there are almost no vehicles of any kind in sight. Dad had a cousin named Daniel Donahue who lived in Pittsfield and that is why we stopped to visit there. Near Pittsfield, we crossed the Housatonic River that Dad's father once threw him into and told him to swim!?

GRANDFATHER'S "SHANTY IRISH" HOME

At the left in this photograph, you can just see the very distinctive "German silver" radiator of the Oakland parked in front of Dad's grandfather's house in Great Barrington, Massachusetts. He had lived there briefly as a boy and attended the Water Street School. It was certainly no coincidence that Father contrived to route the eastern end of the Yellowstone Trail not only through his own birthplace at Huntington, but also via his cousins at Pittsfield, his mother's relatives at Russell, his mother's grave at Westfield and on to Plymouth where a close uncle lived. This stretch of the Trail is now U.S. Highway 20, which closely follows the route of our 1914 trip.

Commonwealth of Massachusetts.

UNITED STATES OF AMERICA.

CERTIFICATE OF BIRTH.

Town of Huntington, Massachusetts.

June 19th 19/9

I, *Geo W Ford*, hereby certify that I have examined the Records of Births in said Town and find recorded therein the Birth of *Michael Dowling*

The record is in the following words and figures, to wit:

DATE OF BIRTH, *Feb 17 – 1866*

NAME AND SURNAME OF CHILD, *Michael Dowling*

COLOR, — SEX, *Male* CONDITION,

PLACE OF BIRTH, *Huntington*

NAMES OF PARENTS, *John Dowling & (Hanora Bary) Dowling*

RESIDENCE OF PARENTS, *Huntington*

OCCUPATION OF FATHER, *Carpenter*

BIRTHPLACE OF FATHER, *Ireland*

BIRTHPLACE OF MOTHER, *Ireland*

I, *Geo W Ford* above named, depose and say, that I hold the office of Town Clerk of HUNTINGTON, County of HAMPSHIRE, Commonwealth of Massachusetts: that the Records of Births, Marriages and Deaths in the said Town are in my custody, and that the above is a true extract from the Record of Births in said Town, as certified by me.

WITNESS my hand and seal of the said Town on the day and year first above written.

(SEAL)

Geo W Ford.
Town Clerk.

Registered Dec 26 – 1866 (OVER)

[68]

TO THE TOP OF THE BERKSHIRES

There was much excitement and anticipation as we drove up the Jacob's Ladder Trail toward Dad's boyhood home at Huntington, MA. The road over the Berkshires was supposed to be a model highway for automobiles, but I thought it was just as steep as some of the roads out West. We were warned to watch out for spots where a local farmer kept the road muddy, just so he could make money pulling out cars that became stuck. This made  Dad angry and when he got angry, he made everyone jump. This may be the reason why the Yellowstone Trail was routed elsewhere for awhile. ***

This is a photograph of Dad, Kathleen and me at the stone monument which was placed there in 1910 to mark the summit of the Jacob's Ladder Trail and celebrate its opening. Today, this is U.S. Highway 20 and just a scenic byway. Most east-west travel is now via the Massachusetts Turnpike.

*** NOTE: Dorothy never said, but her cousin Barbara Bordewich Witt claimed to have been told the Oakland became stuck in mud and Mr. Dowling had to pay for towing.

BIG ROCK IN FRONT OF SCHOOL HOUSE

My father went to school in the early grades at Russell Mills, MA which is right next to Huntington. He told us that this big out-cropping of rock in front of the school had seemed like a mountain when he was a boy. But it was nothing compared to those real mountains I had seen out West. And, the "ol' swimmin' hole" was no better than our beach at Lake Kandiyohi. Kathleen and Marjorie climbed to the top of Dad's big rock so I could take this snapshot.

Although he attended school here for just a few grades, it was here that he absorbed the history of Massachusetts and the American Revolution. Here that he read about the Minutemen and the Battle of Bunker Hill and the first Thanksgiving after the Mayflower landed at Plymouth Rock. And, where all of the children memorized poems like "The Ride of Paul Revere."

AUNT MARY BARRY'S FARM

Aunt Mary Barry was actually a sister-in-law of Dad's mother. She had been married to his mother's oldest brother, but was now a widow and lived on a farm overlooking the Westfield River in Huntington, MA. Aunt Mary led us up a hill where we all picked wild blueberries and had a wonderful, scenic view of the whole valley and countryside. Dad climbed right up that blueberry hill with us until he found a good picking spot where he could just sit and fill his pail. Soon we had picked enough for several pies! Mary's son Charles and grandson John Spooner also helped pick that day.

ALONG THE FREEDOM TRAIL

Boston was a great eastern city, rich in Colonial history. Dad showed us around on a looping route which he called the "Freedom Trail." Starting from Boston Common, we saw where the American Revolution began at the site of the

Boston Massacre, Old South Meeting House, Faneuil Hall, the Paul Revere House, Old North Church, Boston Harbor and other historic landmarks. We even saw the Fish Market where live lobsters and other kinds of sea creatures were displayed for sale.

Then, Mother and we shopped while Dad went to visit newspaper offices or to meet with automobile enthusiasts, businessmen and politicians. Boston was by far the largest city I had yet seen. The constant activity, unfamiliar faces and strange sounding accents left me feeling a bit bewildered. It was all so very different from anything I had known.

However, it was fun to see the fashions and what women in Boston were wearing. I think Mother purchased some costume jewelry for herself and Kathleen and also bought a summer hat with a veil. Marjorie was the most clothes conscious and bought something for herself, too. I was always jealous of her beauty and thought I was the ugly ducking.

After shopping, Mother found us a place to eat and we enjoyed our own "Boston Tea Party." We stayed at a hotel in Boston for two or three nights.

The Bunker Hill monument and "Old Ironsides" were both across on the opposite side of the Charles River. Dad promised to take us over there after we got back from motoring down to Plymouth, which was not much more than an hour's drive away.

THE DOWLINGS LAND AT PLYMOUTH

From Boston, we motored down to Plymouth, where Dad's uncle Vincent Dowling lived at 8 Murray Street. I don't think the two of them had seen each other for years until we showed up that day. Uncle Vincent had long been employed at the Plymouth Woolen Company as a weaver. Dad had once lived with his family while his own mother lay dying of tuberculosis. Those were sad days, but Dad always made friends easily and was bright in school. Vincent was an older teenager at the time, but remembered going with Dad to his mother's funeral. I took this photograph of Uncle Vincent's house, but somehow failed to get a picture of him or his wife Joanna. I don't believe they had any children.

While in Plymouth, we saw the harbor, the pilgrim monument and the oldest, original stone on the pilgrim burial hill. I had tried to imagine myself coming ashore from the Mayflower, but felt a little disappointed when I finally saw Plymouth Rock. I guess I had been expecting something more impressive and thus didn't even take a snapshot. However, I did purchase a glass paperweight souvenir, molded in the shape and texture of the rock, with the date 1620. It was a nice memento to bring back home and perhaps to school.

PAPA TAKES THE LONG WAY HOME...AGAIN!

Before leaving Boston, we saw Bunker Hill and followed the ride of Paul Revere. Then, we drove up the Atlantic Coast to Gloucester and saw the fishing boats and watched the fishermen clean fish. We visited the Davis Fish Company canning plant and Mother made arrangements for a case of their fish to be sent to us in Olivia. For years after that, she had an order every winter. There was New England clam chowder, lobster, tuna, crabmeat, sardines, minced clams and cod fish. Always of superior quality and we loved it. We made a brief stop and all got out to see the ocean while Dad paid a call on his friend, ex-President Taft at his Beverly Farms summer home.

Proceeding across a bit of New Hampshire and into Maine, we stopped at Ogunquit Beach where we walked barefoot in the sand, waded in the water and climbed among the rocks before enjoying lunch at one of the famous beachfront hotels with its spacious grounds and seaside view. I took this photograph which shows the beach and sand with the tide out.

AT MONUMENT SQUARE IN PORTLAND, MAINE

I took this snapshot of our car circling the "War of the Rebellion" memorial on Congress Street to show the many other cars and traffic in the background. A 3-story brick house nearby was the birthplace and boyhood home of the poet Henry Wadsworth Longfellow. Portland was the largest city in Maine, but much smaller than Boston. Brick sidewalks and cobblestone streets led down a steep hill to the waterfront where all kinds of boats were docked alongside the piers. We stayed at a hotel overlooking the bay and found a good restaurant where we ate "shore dinner" with lobster and all of the fixings.

WE TASTE THAT POLAND SPRINGS WATER

After a good night's sleep, we left Portland and drove up to Poland Springs, which was famous for its pure, clean drinking water. I remember that, on the way, we crossed over a river on a covered wooden bridge.

We visited the Spring House at Poland Springs and tasted a dipper-full of that water which Dad insisted was so very "splendid." It did taste cold and refreshing, but I doubted that it was any better than spring water we had back home.

After staying overnight at Poland Springs, we drove over to Bartlett, NH on a very scenic route and on through the Green Mountains and White Mountains on a different road back to Buffalo. We stopped, picked berries, bought cream and sugar and bread that was our lunch, high on a hilltop looking at the simply gorgeous countryside. It was a leisurely trip as I recall, because we always seemed to be stopping to see something, or resting by the roadside, or taking a walk through the woods or visiting somebody. This snapshot is a spare tire view of the Oakland stopped for a "rest" before Crawford Notch, NH.

It was all picturesque. We went through the Indian historical country and had a boat ride on Lake Champlain. Then Dad told us there was one more, very spectacular place we had to see before we boarded our ship for home. Niagara Falls!

AN AMAZING SPECTACLE

Niagara Falls was an awe-inspiring, natural wonder. This, rather poor, black and white photograph doesn't begin to show what a really commanding spectacle it was. I thought the thundering white water cascade was both frightening and beautiful. I saw all of the lovely colors of the rainbow sparkling in clouds of mist. But, I couldn't imagine why anybody would want to risk their life going over the falls in a barrel!?

As I watched the incredibly powerful current, Dad strode over, put his good right arm around me and shouted, "We enjoyed ourselves, didn't we, Dorothy?" "Yes, Papa," I agreed. And, I have been thankful all of my life for those good memories.

CRUISING HOME ON THE SS TIONESTA

Our voyage back to Duluth, aboard the SS Tionesta, was relaxing and uneventful. I was glad not to be riding in that windy car for awhile. The sun was shining, the waves calm and our passage smooth. I mostly napped, read or walked the promenade deck for exercise. Since we had been on that ship before, we knew some of the officers and crew and Dad arranged for us to visit the bridge, where the Captain showed us various charts and instruments and we watched the helmsman at the huge ship's wheel as he kept us on our compass course.

The Oakland was off-loaded at Duluth and we drove from there by way of Superior, Spooner and Hudson, Wisconsin back to St. Paul and Minneapolis. It was good to see familiar sights again as we drove west on Excelsior Boulevard to the city of Excelsior, past Lake Minnetonka and along the Yellowstone Trail as it wound through the rural countryside toward Olivia.

It was late in the evening of August 29th when Dad turned the Oakland into our driveway on DePue Avenue. It was a very quiet homecoming, compared to the summer before. Dad didn't honk or parade up Main Street and no crowd was assembled to greet us. Just Aunt Hattie, Gram, one or two close neighbors and, of course, the dogs who were very glad to see us.

Our trip had covered nearly 5,000 miles. I was pleased to be home again, safe and sound!

Route of
Yellowstone Trail

Maine

Vermont

New York

New Hampshire

Portland

Schenectaty

Massachusetts

Boston

Lake Ontario

Cooperstown

Albany

Pittsfield

Jacob's

Plymouth

Niagra Falls
Buffalo

Huntington

Springfield

Connecticut

Lake
Erie

Appendix

THE BOY WHO WAS FROZEN...

December 4, 1880

Young Michael Dowling started out to say good-bye to his pony, but was jolted off the wagon he was riding on, then left behind and lost in a 50-below zero Minnesota blizzard. Here's the true story of how he survived the storm, as told by Kathleen Dowling, and why it astonished everyone that he didn't die.

"One afternoon in December, Mike jumped on a soap box in the back of a lumber wagon which two men were going to drive to the farm at which his pony was kept. Mike loved that pony and he would not leave Canby, MN until he had seen that it was well cared for. Mike was then fourteen years old, strong, active, husky.

The two men and the boy jogged along in the December darkness, happy and content. Mike was thinking about school, about his friends, about his pony (Charlie). He was startled when one of the men called,

'Look out there! We're meeting a storm head-on!'

It was true. By twisting his neck around, Mike could see the gray wall which meant a blizzard and a bad one. Soon the storm was upon them. The snow was blinding as it drove furiously over the un-fenced fields. The horses were trying to find their way to their old home; the driver trying to stay in the direction of the farm. Neither the man nor the horse could see; neither knew what he was doing or where he was going. The man became excited and whipped up his horse. Suddenly they careened into a plowed field. At the moment the wagon struck the first furrow, Mike was thrown off the back. He was stunned by the fall, but in a moment he was up

> *Lost in a -50 below zero blizzard, Mike searched for shelter*

and running frantically after the wagon. He cried out at the top of his voice but the men could not hear him above the howl of the storm and the noise of the wagon wheels on the frozen ground. Mike tried to keep in the tracks, but he had to feel for them with his hands and soon even that faint help was obliterated by the snow. Undaunted, he started to find the railroad. He was so hopelessly lost that he could not find it. By that time his hair was thick and his face and hands ached with the cold. He staggered around in the blizzard hoping to find a farm house in which he could get shelter from the storm. After a long time, he came to a woodpile. That meant a house nearby.

Mike climbed to the top of the pile and, taking sticks of wood, threw them one by one in every direction, hoping to hear the sound of the impact on the wall of the house. He heard nothing. Then he climbed down and, taking an armful of wood, walked straight against the wind for about fifty feet. There he threw wood in each direction. He did this many times, judging his position by the direction of the wind. Every time he kept one stick to throw back at the pile so that he would find it again. Then one time he did not hit the pile. He had to hunt for the woodpile and he could not find it.

He struggled blindly until he happened to strike a straw pile. This meant some shelter so he dug his way in, head first. There he felt comfortable – and drowsy. He was enough of a Minnesotan to know that he must keep awake or he would freeze. He felt the waves of bitter cold which started at his ankles and twisted upward around his body like a corkscrew.

Finally he decided that his long night must be over. He put his head out of the straw pile and saw the red sun just above the horizon. And there, not more than half a mile away, was a familiar farmhouse!

Overjoyed, he jumped up. He could not stand. He tried again and again, but each time he fell. His legs were like sticks of ice. He could see them, but he could feel no sensation at all in them. He realized then that his feet were frozen; he clapped his hands together and it sounded as if he had struck two pieces of wood together! They, too, were frozen. He kept jumping up and falling down until he reached the farmhouse. He did as well as if he had been walking on stilts. Within two feet of the door he saw two sticks of wood: he had come that close to being saved!

Mike went into the farmhouse. The woman there called the doctor and with the help of others around the farm, they thawed out Mike's legs and arms. As he told me afterwards, "Being frozen is not pleasant; but being unfrozen is a decidedly painful operation."

**

As soon as the storm had passed, Michael was moved into the James Larson house in Canby, MN. When signs of gangrene appeared, a surgeon was called who drove 35-miles by horse and sleigh to come and amputate in a desperate attempt to save the boy's life. The surgeon, Dr. Andrews of Marshall, MN had done many amputations on Civil War battlefields and was one of the most experienced doctors of his time.

The operation was performed by the light of a kerosene lamp, hung above a kitchen table covered with oil cloth and the local drug store had not enough chloroform to last. By the end of the long operation, it took three men to hold Michael down as he fought and screamed in an agony of pain. It was a wonder that he didn't die.

> **He had surgery on a kitchen table by light of a kerosene lamp**

That was a terrible winter for everyone in the village. The days were dark. The streets were silent. The houses of the settlers were buried in snow so deep that people had to climb up and over drifts to venture in or out. Firewood was scarce. Telegraph poles and fence posts were chopped down and burned. People in sod houses slept under buffalo robes or carpet to keep warm. Even the railroad was drifted closed. For three months, not a single train came through town.

During those dark days, as young Michael lay in bed waiting for his stumps to heal, it became clear to him that "there was just one thing for me to do if I did not have any legs or arms, and that was to polish up the machinery above the neck."

He resolved, passionately, to "learn how to learn" and get an education!

...AND HIS STARTLING PROPOSAL!

This photo of young Michael J. Dowling was taken in April, 1883 just before he went to "stand on his knees" before the County Commissioners, telling them that he refused to accept welfare or placement in foster care for the rest of his life. Michael's two legs had been amputated six-inches below the knees, his left arm below the elbow and all fingers and part of the thumb from his right hand. He wore no artificial limbs for his appearance before the members of the Board; just a pair of leather pads so that he could shuffle about without hurting his knees.

Refusing welfare, the boy offered to make a startling bargain with the County officials. Smiling and looking the Chairman straight in the eye, he said, "If you will give me one year at Carleton College it will never cost this county another cent as long as I live to keep me going."

"But, you can't back that up; that is just your say so," the Chairman objected.

"Well," the boy answered, "I mean it."

The Board felt that "red headed Irish kid" had a lot of brass, but his heart was honest, his head on straight, his courage very strong and his word as good as gold. Mike had been cowboying on his own and independently self-supporting from the age of 12.

A vote to accept the deal and send the boy to college was passed the next day, two votes for and one against.

Thus began his years of inspiring courage and achievement!

MICHAEL THE "WOODEN MAN"

Renville Circa 1892-1902

With an artificial arm and two wooden legs, Michael was sometimes called the "Wooden Man". Everyone marveled at his courage and all he was able to do. He climbed up and down stairs, danced, rode horseback, pedaled a bicycle, roller skated, was a crack shot and hunted ducks, prairie chickens and moose, walked long distances, wrote with excellent penmanship and even taught himself to operate a typewriter and type with two "fingers".

The last thing Dorothy would hear at night was her father climbing up the stairs and turning out the lights. There were no handicap ramps or lifts in the Dowling house. Here is a photograph of Michael, taken about 1898, in front of the house where Dorothy was born. The two horses were named "Billy" and "Kid."

MICHAEL THE EDITOR

April 12, 1889, Michael Dowling and John Spencer co-founded The Renville Star newspaper, published every Friday. It claimed to have the largest circulation of any newspaper in the county. M.J. Dowling was Editor. He wrote that "The STAR" is Republican, moral and fearless." Here we see Mike at his roll top desk and typewriter in the newspaper print shop, which was equipped with the newest in presses, type and material. "If you don't like the name of our paper, read it backwards," he quipped. Spencer later married Jennie's sister Anna and became Mike's brother in-law.

While editor, Michael was notified to appear "in the forenoon with shovel to work on the streets and highways of the village."

His answer was to write a scathing editorial that "this is evidence of great administrative ability! What fine roads we have for sure if men without legs or arms are to do the shoveling. Ye, Gods, what thrift!"

In 1900, President McKinley sent Michael to the Philippines. Officially, to inspect the school system. But, secretly, to meet with Army commanders and gather information for the Secretary of War. This photo shows Dowling in Manila wearing a jungle helmet and tropical white suit. When this was taken, the Aguinaldo insurgents had already killed 1,525 Americans; an average of 74 per month.

This photograph shows an Army wagon on the island of Cebu with its armed escort of eight American soldiers. The man up on the wagon box with the driver (back row, left) was probably Dowling. The officer next to him may be the Commanding Officer of the island. The picture appears to have been posed in front of a school building on the day in April, 1900 when the two men inspected classrooms and outposts together.

A HEAVY ARM
AN UNCOMFORTABLE LEG

In summer, during the hottest months of the year, Michael had to get about with two artificial legs and an

Showing tools used in Artificial Hand and Wrist

artificial arm. When he became tired, he would sometimes complain that he had a "heavy arm" or "an uncomfortable leg" where he had rubbed some skin off. He always perspired freely. In summer he wore an alpaca suite that was supposed to be more comfortable. But he would simply drip. He told Dorothy that she could cool off by running cold water onto her wrists. There was no air conditioning in those times.

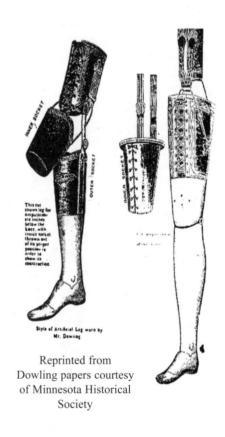

This cut shows leg for amputation six inches below the knee, with inner socket thrown out of its proper position in order to show its construction.

Style of Artificial Leg worn by Mr. Dowling

Reprinted from
Dowling papers courtesy
of Minnesota Historical
Society

MICHAEL THE MECHANIZED MAN...

Renville County 1903

Michael Dowling bought the first "horseless carriage" sold in the county. It was all hand made by his friend Olaus Lende over in Granite Falls and was the first of many early automobiles manufactured and sold by the Lende machine shop. The vehicle had a 2-cylinder engine, chain drive, kerosene lantern headlamps and an air horn with a rubber squeeze bulb to warn pedestrians and others in the way. Top speed was about 10-miles per hour, so it took all day to drive to Minneapolis. Nevertheless, Dowling was thrilled by his primitive machine and called it "Old Norah."

No more was he the "Wooden Man." Now he called himself "Michael the Mechanized Man" and drove that car all around the countryside, while enjoying an exhilarating new feeling of freedom and mobility. In this photograph, we see his mud spattered "horseless carriage" in front of the E.H. Erickson Artificial Limb Company in Minneapolis. His passenger was Mr. E. Hugo Erickson, a long time friend and benefactor who outfitted Mike with his artificial limbs.

The curved front of the car opened up for a back and foot rest to accommodate two more riders. Dorothy recalled that "Dad once raced a White Steamer down Excelsior Boulevard in Minneapolis and won! But, Mother lost all of her hairpins during the race and all of our tools flew out of the storage box. I held on to Dad's coat pocket so I wouldn't fall out."

It was a long, narrow road winding through the prairies to Minneapolis. It frightened Dorothy to drive at night and see wildfires burning in the distance.

HE WAS FASTER THAN DAN PATCH!

The Olivia Times, October 29, 1903, printed this amusing bit of local news:

#

#   #

M.J. Dowling and M.C. Kemp "automobubbled" up the road as far as Renville, last Thursday, and the natives of Danube held their different breaths (and that's saying a great deal when you consider how strong they were) as the automobile went tearing down their main street at a faster pace than that set by Dan Patch. A little ways out of Renville there was a bizz-, bazz-, buzz-, and the machine came to a standstill and remained so until the chauffeur (that's Dutch for Dowling) and his partner in misery made some repairs which consumed close to an hour. About this time a farmer (a friend of Dowling's before he got the auto) drove out in the field in order to get around, and with snorts of laughter, mingled with a tone of fine irony, shouted, "I hope that _ _ _ breaks down every mile you go, and it takes an hour to fix it." But it didn't, and this added insult to injury was soon only a faint memory.

#

#   #

NOTE: Dan Patch was the name of a very famous horse.
       The fastest pacer of his day.

HE WAS A BUILDER OF ROADS

Olivia, MN 1905

There was once a certain mile-long stretch of road that ran across a low place outside of Olivia and became almost impassable during rainy seasons. In 1905 Michael Dowling decided to do something about that always wet and muddy road.

As written in the Minneapolis Sunday Tribune, "Mr. Dowling obtained free of cost enough granite from the state reformatory at St. Cloud to put a solid roadbed through the marsh. He got the railroads interested in the project to such an extent that they delivered trainloads of this granite in Olivia without charge." When the work was done, Dowling had a hard surface highway that was almost as good as paved, but cost little more than an ordinary dirt grade.

Some were against paying taxes to build new two-lane roads for people who could afford automobiles.

"What for do you hafta' build a two-lane road?" one farmer objected. "You can only go in one direction."

"Ya," agreed his neighbor. "And if you meet another car, then for sure you can always pull over and stop and wait for them to get by." In those times, nobody could imagine roads jammed with automobiles and two-way traffic.

When another farmer plowed up the dirt road past his home in protest, Dowling invited the man and his family to come for a Sunday drive in his car. At first he took them along a good, smooth road and the wife and children were having a grand time. But, on the way back, Dowling drove just as fast over the road that the farmer had plowed up and the family had to hang on tight or be jolted out of their seats. Nothing was said, but within a week, the farmer had restored that plowed up road to smooth driving condition.

With the support of Dowling's farmer friends, it wasn't long before Renville County won national recognition for having the best roads in Minnesota and Michael the best highway builder. He became an enthusiastic member of the Minneapolis Automobile Club and President of the Minneapolis "Good Roads" Association. When the Yellowstone Trail Association was formed in 1912, Dowling was named to the executive committee and played a key role in bringing Minnesota into that organization.

This photo was probably taken during the Glidden tour from St. Paul to Sioux Falls in 1910. Dowling is the man wearing a cap with visor (sixth from the right). The trophy for best roads during the tour was awarded to Renville County and presented by Louis Hill, President of the Great Northern Railroad.

A WINNING SLOGAN FOR THE TRAIL

Michael Dowling knew how to sell a grand idea or vision! And, having a winning slogan was one of the most important ways.

So, in February 1915, when members of the Trail Association heard him speak at their annual meeting about his trip to Plymouth Rock and the pledges of support he had received, it was quickly moved to drop the words "Twin Cities, Aberdeen and Park" from the name of the organization and replace them with the official name and slogan proposed by Dowling: "Yellowstone Trail, A Good Road From Plymouth Rock to Puget Sound." Thus began the transformation of the association into a truly nationwide enterprise.

Dowling had learned long ago, that any idea had to be sold not only on its benefits and what it had to offer of real and lasting value, but also on future expectations and romance. So, the Trail was not just a road for automobiles, or a road to open the West. It was the highway to a golden future. For this was the dawn of the automobile age with incredible changes and opportunities ahead!

The Opera House in Montevideo, Minnesota was chosen for the February meeting-place because of its convenient proximity both to South Dakota and to Dowling's home in Olivia. The distance between the two towns was only 35 miles. But, in winter, most of the delegates stored their automobiles and did not drive. So, like the others, Michael commuted to the event by rail.

INDIANS HELPED BUILD THE YELLOWSTONE TRAIL

Although Michael J. Dowling may have become lost on the Standing Rock Indian Reservation, he certainly knew his way around the halls of Washington, D.C. The Olivia Times, June 21, 1917 printed this report about how he used his political influence to have a good road built across that trackless, open prairie.

#

#   #

Last Monday, Indian Agent Kitch of the Standing Rock Agency took all Indians available from Yates, Wakpala, Little Eagle and Bull Head for road work, forming two camps with tractors, one at the east end and one at the west end of the reservation to work on the Yellowstone Trail from Mobridge to McIntosh. Three bridge crews are also at work building bridges on the reservation. The work will be completed July 15th. This is a result of Mr. Dowling's visit to the Commissioner of Indian Affairs at Washington.

President McKinley ↑   ↑ **Michael Dowling**

Photo of Dowling with President McKinley and members of Republican league on President's front porch in Canton, Ohio 1897. Dowling is front row, second to right from the President.

THE BEST ORGANIZED ROAD ASSOCIATION

In 1917, Michael Dowling was elected President of the Yellowstone Trail Association, succeeding trail founder Joe Parmley. He immediately began to reshape it into what some called the best organized road association in America. As a result of his inspiration and leadership:

• The motto "A Good Road from Plymouth Rock to Puget Sound" was officially adopted as the slogan of the Trail.

• Trail headquarters was moved from South Dakota to the Andrus Building in downtown Minneapolis and his friend H.O. Cooley installed as general manager.

• The Trail was re-marked under a uniform system and designated for federal, state and county funding. Uniform traffic rules were adopted.

• Tours of the Trail were planned for governors, magazine writers and other guests.

• A network of free tourist information bureaus was planned and the first opened in Chicago, Minneapolis, Miles City and Seattle.

• A huge quantity of touring maps and literature was printed and distributed to auto clubs and motoring enthusiasts.

During these significant war-time years, it was Dowling's genius for organization, good humor and knowledge that transformed the Yellowstone Trail from a more or less local effort, linking up roads in the West, into a true, nationwide enterprise.

When in 1917, a military dispatch was relayed by automobile along the Yellowstone Trail from Plymouth Rock to Seattle in the record time of 121-hours and 12-minutes, the Trail became recognized as the main automobile route across the northern states and one of the four major American east/west highways of its time.

At the conclusion of his term, Dowling was honored at a dinner held in Chicago during the 1918 convention of all the National Highway Associations. The dining room and tables were decorated with green napkins and shamrocks and a band played Irish songs. Dowling was presented with a silver loving cup as a token of appreciation and esteem and, true to his reputation as "the world's greatest optimist," responded with a prediction that the entire Yellowstone Trail was likely to be paved within the next five years.

Bibliography

1. Michael J. Dowling. A story of rehabilitation by a cripple who is not a cripple. Annals of the American Academy of Political and Social Science. (November 1918): 43-50

2. John Culbert Faries. A Biography of Michael J. Dowling, unpublished manuscript at Minnesota History Center received from Henrietta "Hattie" Bordewich December 17, 1943.

3. Prudence Tasker Olsen. As I knew Dowling. Minneapolis Journal September 10, 1921.

4. Elizabeth McLeod Jones. Renville County Man Pronounced Best Highway Worker. Minneapolis Journal September 5, 1915.

5. Alice A. and John Wm. Ridge. Introducing the Yellowstone Trail. (Altoona, Wisconsin: Yellowstone Trail Publishers 2000).

6. Olivia Times. October 29, 1903.

7. Livingston Daily Enterprise. July 16, 1913.

8. Olivia Times. June 21, 1917.

9. Dowling. Michael J. and Jennie B. Papers, 1883-1944. Minnesota Historical Society. Microfilm rolls 1 and 2.

10. On the Yellowstone Trail. A reproduction of the first year book of the Yellowstone Trail Association 1914. Alice and John Ridge (Altoona, Wisconsin, Yellowstone Trail Publishers 2003).

11. Adrian Bottge. Adrian Looks Back (Renville, Minnesota. Renville Star Farmer and the Historic Renville Preservation Committee 1988).

12. Ida Windhorst. Letter to Kathleen Dowling dated April 20, 1974. Copy, some pages missing.

13. Dorothy Dowling Prichard. Memories. (Typed spiral bound) and copyright 1980 pages 55-60 at al.

14. Jacob's Ladder Trail Scenic Byway, Inc. Steve Hamlin, Chairman. Jacob's Ladder Trail (Map and brochure). Huntington, MA 1991.

15. History of the Yellowstone Trail Association and the Good Roads of Renville County 1910-1917. Renville County Historical Museum, Morton, MN (25 pages stapled) 2007.

16. Montevideo Leader. February 25-March 5, 1915.